RONALDO

A STORY OF HARD WORK AND DETERMINATION

This book belongs to

_____

CONTENTS

CHAPTER 1

A Humble Beginning

In a small village on the island of Madeira, Portugal, Ronaldo was born into a modest and hardworking family. Life was not easy for young Ronaldo. He shared a small room with his three siblings, and their home was filled with love, but also with financial struggles.

Ronaldo's father faced his own battles with alcoholism, which added an extra layer of challenge to their already difficult circumstances. Despite the hardships he faced at home, Ronaldo found solace and joy in playing soccer. From a young age, he displayed an incredible passion for the game.

With no fancy equipment or extravagant facilities, Ronaldo and his friends would gather in the narrow streets of their neighborhood, using anything they could find as makeshift goalposts. Whether it was a pair of shoes, a pile of clothes, or even rocks, nothing would dampen their enthusiasm for playing the beautiful game.

While Ronaldo's family struggled to make ends meet, his mother, a hardworking cleaner, always encouraged his love for soccer. She saw the joy it brought him and recognized his talent. Despite the limited resources available to them, she did everything she could to support his dreams.

In those early years, Ronaldo would spend countless hours honing his skills. He would dribble a worn-out ball through the narrow alleys and squares, showcasing his determination and natural talent. Even at a young age, his dedication and focus set him apart from his peers.

Ronaldo's love for soccer was like a flame burning brightly within him, driving him forward. It was on those dusty streets of Madeira that he began to develop the skills that would one day make him a football legend.

Little did young Ronaldo know that these humble beginnings would be the foundation of his incredible journey. His unwavering love for the game and his unyielding determination would carry him far beyond the narrow streets of his childhood village. As he continued to grow, so did his dreams of becoming one of the greatest footballers the world had ever seen.

And so, with each kick of the ball, Ronaldo's journey began, fueled by his passion and nurtured by his unwavering dedication. The story of a boy with a dream was just beginning, and the world would soon bear witness to the remarkable tale of hard work and determination that would shape his destiny.

The Boy at Sporting Lisbon

At the age of 10, Ronaldo's talent caught the attention of scouts from Sporting Lisbon, one of Portugal's most prestigious youth teams. They witnessed his lightning-fast footwork, his impeccable ball control, and his ability to score goals with precision. Recognizing his potential, they extended an invitation to join their academy.

The news filled Ronaldo's heart with excitement and a sense of validation. It was a testament to the countless hours he had poured into his craft. The opportunity to train with some of the best young players in the country was a stepping stone towards his ultimate goal: becoming a professional soccer player.

Upon joining the academy, Ronaldo found himself in a new environment filled with talented players and experienced coaches. It was an opportunity for him to further refine his skills, deepen his understanding of the game, and grow as a player. Ronaldo embraced the intense training sessions, absorbing knowledge from his mentors, and honing his abilities.

At the academy, Ronaldo's commitment to hard work and improvement was evident to all. He would arrive early and stay late, tirelessly practicing his dribbling, shooting, and tactical awareness. He recognized that this was a crucial period for his development, and he was determined to make the most of it.

Under the guidance of the academy coaches, Ronaldo's skills flourished. His speed, agility, and technical proficiency caught the attention of his teammates and coaches alike. He began to stand out as a player with tremendous potential, marked by his exceptional performances in training and friendly matches.

As Ronaldo's talent continued to blossom, the moment he had been eagerly awaiting finally arrived – his debut for Sporting Lisbon's first team. It was a dream come true for the young prodigy. Stepping onto the pitch in the iconic green and white jersey, Ronaldo felt a mixture of excitement and nerves.

The match proved to be a test of Ronaldo's abilities and mental fortitude. He was up against seasoned professionals and faced the pressure of performing on the grand stage. However, Ronaldo's determination shone through as he displayed his skills and fearlessly took on defenders.

In his debut, Ronaldo left an indelible mark. His speed, agility, and electrifying dribbling ability captivated the crowd and impressed both teammates and opponents. Although he may not have scored in that match, his presence on the field and the impact he made were undeniable.

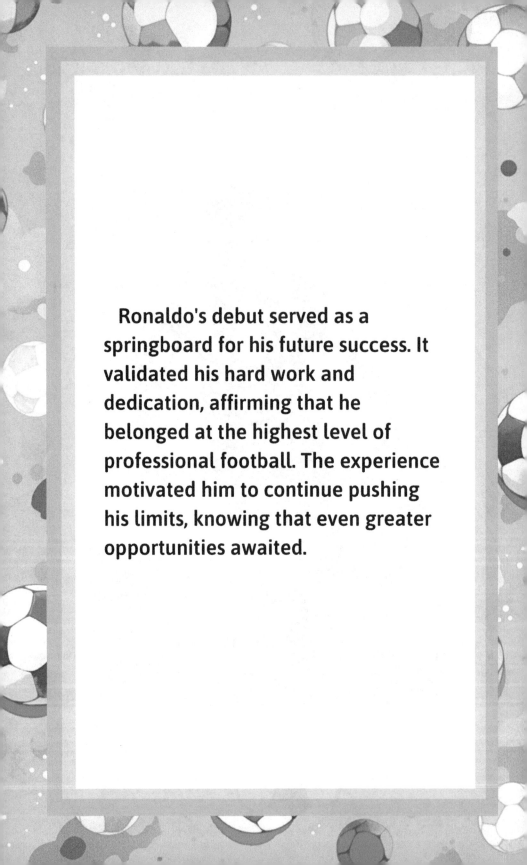

Ronaldo's debut served as a springboard for his future success. It validated his hard work and dedication, affirming that he belonged at the highest level of professional football. The experience motivated him to continue pushing his limits, knowing that even greater opportunities awaited.

As Ronaldo's reputation grew, his performances caught the attention of talent scouts from top clubs across Europe. Coaches and scouts were impressed by his raw talent, work ethic, and versatility on the field. Word began to spread about this young prodigy who possessed immense potential.

Clubs from different countries began to express interest in acquiring Ronaldo's services. Their representatives attended his matches, observing his skills, assessing his suitability for their team, and envisioning the impact he could make in their respective leagues. The attention from these clubs signaled Ronaldo's imminent ascent to the pinnacle of professional soccer.

CHAPTER 3

Becoming a Superstar

The transfer to Manchester United marked a turning point in Ronaldo's career. His move to one of the world's most prestigious clubs offered him the platform to showcase his immense talent on a grand stage. Ronaldo's arrival at Old Trafford was met with excitement and anticipation, as fans eagerly awaited the impact he would make.

It didn't take long for Ronaldo to make his mark at Manchester United. His explosive pace, impeccable dribbling, and thunderous shots became the talk of the football world. Ronaldo's performances on the pitch were nothing short of spectacular, electrifying stadiums and leaving defenders in awe.

With Ronaldo's contributions, Manchester United experienced a period of unprecedented success. His relentless pursuit of excellence played a vital role in the team's trophy triumphs. Together with his teammates, Ronaldo won numerous domestic league titles, domestic cups, and even the prestigious UEFA Champions League.

As Ronaldo's star rose, the world began to take notice. His outstanding performances and natural charisma captured the hearts of fans worldwide. Ronaldo's unique playing style, characterized by his flair, agility, and ability to score from almost any position, made him a player like no other. His combination of skill, speed, and strength set him apart from his peers and made him a true standout.

Ronaldo's rise to stardom went beyond the football pitch. His marketability and global appeal grew exponentially, turning him into a brand in his own right. Sponsors clamored to associate themselves with Ronaldo, recognizing his influence and immense popularity. His image graced billboards, commercials, and magazine covers, cementing his status as a global icon.

Amidst the recognition and accolades, Ronaldo remained grounded and dedicated to his craft. He never rested on his laurels and constantly sought ways to improve his game. His tireless work ethic and commitment to perfection became synonymous with his name, inspiring aspiring young footballers around the world.

CHAPTER 4

Obtaining Greatness

With his sights set on new horizons, Ronaldo made a historic transfer to Real Madrid, the Spanish powerhouse. The transfer broke records and raised expectations to unprecedented heights. With the iconic white jersey adorning his shoulders, Ronaldo took on the challenge of leading one of the most storied clubs in football history.

At Real Madrid, Ronaldo wasted no time in leaving his mark. His goal-scoring prowess was unparalleled, and his hunger for success was insatiable. Season after season, Ronaldo shattered records and propelled Real Madrid to new heights. He became the club's all-time leading goal scorer, surpassing legends who had come before him.

One of Ronaldo's greatest achievements at Real Madrid was his role in securing multiple UEFA Champions League titles. His performances in Europe's most prestigious club competition were nothing short of sensational.

Ronaldo's ability to perform on the biggest stage and deliver in crucial moments cemented his legacy as one of the greatest players to have graced the tournament.

Alongside team success, Ronaldo's individual accomplishments continued to accumulate. He earned numerous individual accolades, including multiple FIFA Ballon d'Or awards, which recognized him as the best player in the world.

His remarkable consistency, exceptional skills, and unwavering drive propelled him to the forefront of the footballing world.

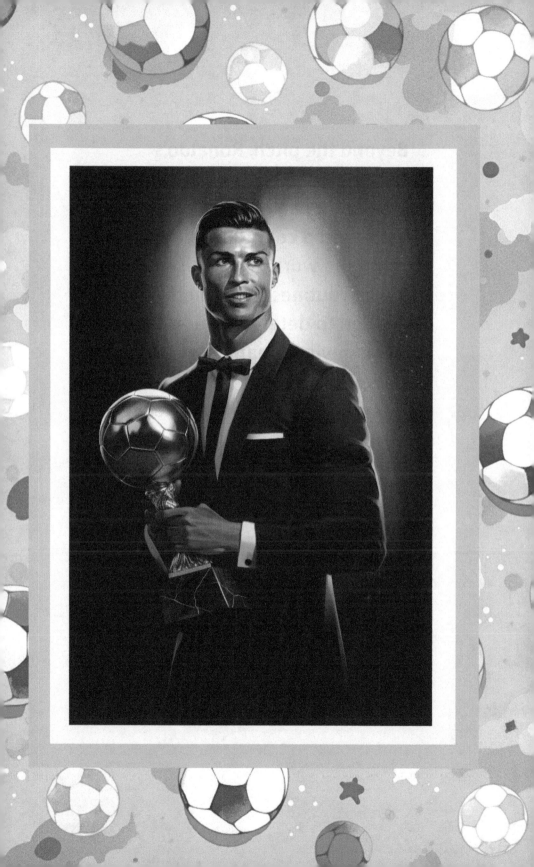

Beyond the pitch, Ronaldo's influence extended far and wide. His success story and dedication to his craft inspired countless young players around the world. From his relentless training routines to his meticulous attention to detail, Ronaldo showed that achieving greatness requires a combination of talent, hard work, and a relentless pursuit of excellence.

Ronaldo's impact transcended football, as he used his platform to support charitable initiatives and make a difference in the lives of those less fortunate. His philanthropic endeavors served as a testament to his character, emphasizing the importance of giving back and making a positive impact on society.

CHAPTER 5

The National Hero

Ronaldo's journey as a national hero began when he first donned the iconic red and green jersey of the Portuguese national team. From the moment he stepped onto the international stage, his presence and influence were undeniable.

Ronaldo's commitment to representing his country with passion and excellence resonated with fans and instilled a sense of belief and hope.

One of Ronaldo's defining moments with the Portuguese national team was their triumph in the European Championship. Leading the team as captain, Ronaldo played a pivotal role in guiding Portugal to their first major international trophy.

His performances throughout the tournament were exceptional, inspiring his teammates and electrifying stadiums.

Ronaldo's ability to elevate his game on the international stage was evident in his remarkable goal-scoring record for Portugal. He became the country's all-time leading goal scorer, surpassing previous records with remarkable consistency. His passion, skill, and leadership made him a talismanic figure for the national team.

Beyond the European Championship, Ronaldo's influence on the Portuguese national team extended to other international successes. He played a vital role in securing qualification for major tournaments and led the team to strong performances in events such as the FIFA World Cup. Ronaldo's presence alone commanded respect from opponents and brought a sense of belief to his teammates.

The pride and admiration Ronaldo receives from his country are immeasurable. His achievements have united the Portuguese people, creating a sense of shared joy and triumph. From passionate celebrations in stadiums to cheers erupting in towns and cities across Portugal, the nation rallies behind their hero, grateful for the pride he brings to their country.

Ronaldo's impact transcends football, as he has become an ambassador for Portugal on the global stage. His success story serves as an inspiration to young Portuguese players, igniting dreams and fueling aspirations. Ronaldo's dedication, perseverance, and unwavering love for his country epitomize the qualities that make him a revered figure and a national hero.

CHAPTER 6

Off The Field Effects

Ronaldo's philanthropic endeavors have touched countless lives and exemplify his commitment to making a positive difference in the world. He recognizes the platform and visibility that his fame provides and embraces the opportunity to use it for the betterment of society.

One of the primary focuses of Ronaldo's charitable work is supporting children and youth. Through his foundation and partnerships with various organizations, he aims to improve the lives of disadvantaged children, provide access to education and healthcare, and promote social inclusion. Ronaldo's empathy and compassion drive him to help those in need, particularly the most vulnerable members of society.

Ronaldo's efforts extend far beyond monetary donations. He actively engages with the projects and initiatives he supports, making personal visits, meeting with children and their families, and participating in events and campaigns. His genuine care and connection with those he seeks to help leave a lasting impact on the individuals he encounters.

Using his own journey as inspiration, Ronaldo encourages children to pursue their dreams and believe in themselves. He emphasizes the importance of hard work, dedication, and perseverance in achieving success. By sharing his story, Ronaldo inspires young people to overcome obstacles and strive for greatness, regardless of their circumstances.

Ronaldo also promotes the value of giving back to the community. He encourages individuals to use their talents and resources to make a positive impact on the lives of others. Ronaldo's example serves as a reminder that success should not be measured solely by individual accomplishments but also by the positive influence one can have on society.

Through his philanthropic work, Ronaldo seeks to create a legacy that extends beyond his achievements on the football field. He aims to inspire a new generation of compassionate and socially conscious individuals who will carry on the spirit of giving back.

CHAPTER 7

Lessons from Ronaldo

One of the key lessons to learn from Ronaldo is the importance of discipline. Throughout his career, Ronaldo has shown unwavering commitment to his craft, putting in countless hours of training and maintaining a disciplined lifestyle. He understands that success is not achieved overnight but is the result of consistent effort and dedication.

By adopting a disciplined approach, you can prioritize your goals, establish healthy habits, and work towards your dreams with focus and determination.

Perseverance is another vital lesson Ronaldo teaches us. His journey to success was not without obstacles and setbacks. From facing financial hardships in his early life to encountering challenges on the football pitch, Ronaldo has shown remarkable resilience and the ability to bounce back stronger. He never let failures define him but used them as stepping stones towards improvement.

Embracing perseverance allows you to face challenges head-on, learn from your experiences, and keep pushing forward despite setbacks.

Ronaldo's success is not solely attributed to his individual brilliance but also to his understanding of the value of teamwork. He recognizes that achieving greatness requires working harmoniously with others, respecting their strengths, and leveraging collective efforts. Ronaldo's ability to contribute to the success of his teams serves as a reminder that collaboration and cooperation are essential ingredients for success in any endeavor.

Embracing teamwork fosters a sense of unity, empathy, and the understanding that achieving common goals is often more rewarding than individual achievements.

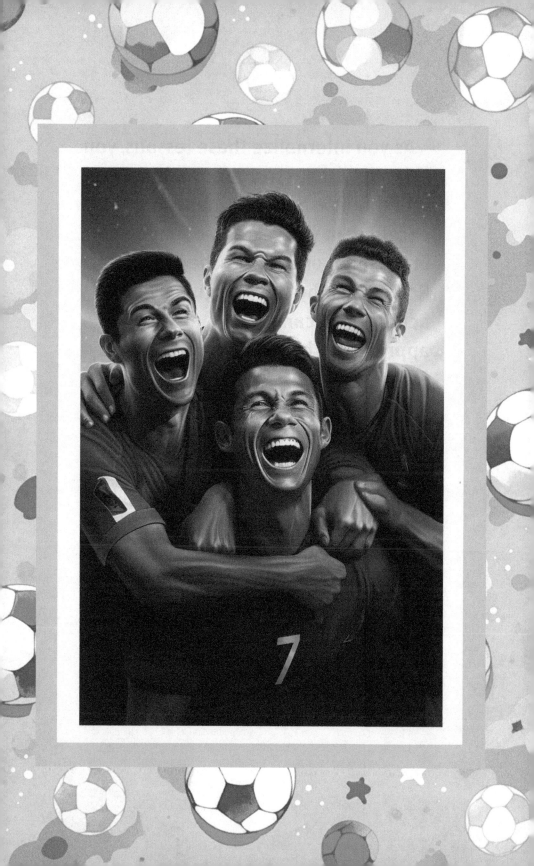

As you internalize these lessons, you can apply them to your own life. Whether it is pursuing a passion, excelling in your career, or engaging in personal endeavors, the values Ronaldo embodies can guide your actions. You can adopt a disciplined approach to hone your skills and stay focused on your goals.

When faced with challenges, you can draw inspiration from Ronaldo's perseverance and continue to strive for improvement. Embracing teamwork enables you to collaborate effectively with others, appreciating the strength in unity and collective effort.

Above all, Ronaldo's story serves as a powerful reminder to chase your dreams relentlessly and never give up. He overcame numerous obstacles to achieve greatness, proving that with hard work, dedication, and belief in yourself, anything is possible.

Ronaldo's journey inspires you to set audacious goals, believe in your own potential, and persevere through adversity.

Your Journey Starts Now

As you reach the end of this book, remember that your journey in soccer starts now. The stories and lessons shared throughout these pages serve as a foundation for your own personal growth and development. Just like Ronaldo, you have the potential to achieve great things on and off the field.

To begin your journey, it's important to embrace the joy and passion that soccer brings. Let your love for the game be the driving force behind your efforts. Find joy in every training session, every match, and every opportunity to improve. Keep in mind that every step you take, no matter how small, contributes to your growth as a player.

Training plays a vital role in your soccer journey. Dedicate yourself to regular practice sessions, focusing on improving your skills, fitness, and tactical understanding. Ronaldo's story reminds us that hard work and discipline are essential ingredients for success.

Set goals for yourself and create a training routine that pushes you to your limits. Remember that consistency is key, and small, incremental improvements over time can lead to significant progress.

Staying motivated can be challenging at times, especially when faced with setbacks or obstacles. It's important to cultivate a strong mindset and a resilient spirit. Ronaldo's journey is a testament to the power of perseverance.

When faced with difficulties, use them as opportunities for growth and learning. Surround yourself with positive influences, such as supportive coaches, teammates, and mentors, who can provide guidance and encouragement along the way.

In closing, Ronaldo has a final message of inspiration for you. He reminds us all that no dream is too big and no goal is out of reach. Believe in yourself and your abilities. Embrace challenges as opportunities for growth. Stay focused, work hard, and never lose sight of your passion. Ronaldo's journey is a testament to the power of perseverance, determination, and unwavering belief in oneself.

Your journey starts now. Embrace it. Cherish it. Make it your own. The world of soccer awaits your presence, your talent, and your unique contribution. Dream big, work hard, and never stop believing in yourself. Let the inspiring story of Cristiano Ronaldo be the catalyst for your own extraordinary soccer journey.

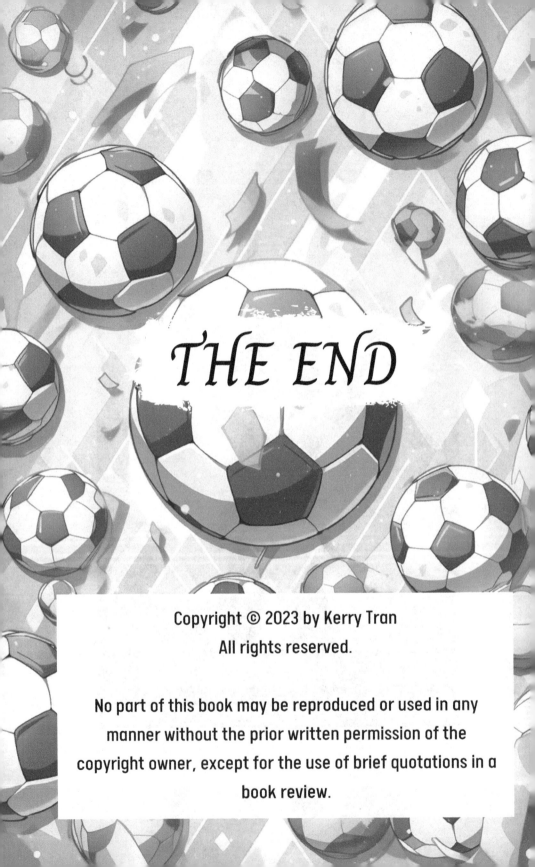

THE END

82579202R00049